The author

GW01458410

Roger James served as a junior officer i (Northumbrian) Di 8th Army's victori nearly to Tunis, and then back ag— equip for the invasion of Sicily in July 1943. They supported, with artillery fire across the Messina straits, the 8th Army's landing on the toe of Italy on 3rd September 1943 - the first invasion of the European continent. Then home to prepare for D-Day. They took part in the invasion of Normandy, and after the break-through there, carried on in the British 2nd Army's advance through northern France and Belgium to Holland. The last action in which he took part at the end of April 1945 was the final liberation of Arnhem. In all these actions he was under the command of General Montgomery who remains for him a great hero.

After the war Roger James returned to Oxford to complete a degree in mathematics and later he became a medical student. Subsequently he was a GP in Portsmouth until 1989 - and from 1973 to 1983 a Portsmouth City Councillor.

Roger James

Montgomery at Normandy

Roger James

TRICORN
BOOKS

Montgomery at Normandy

by Roger James

Design © 131 Design Ltd
www.131design.org
Published by Tricorn Books
www.tricornbooks.co.uk

Typeface:Times
ISBN 978-0-9567597-0-2
Published 2011 by Tricorn Books,
a trading name of 131 Design Ltd.
131 High Street, Old Portsmouth,
PO1 2HW

Printed and bound in Great Britain by

The Complete Product Company Ltd

Montgomery at Normandy

Contents

Chapter 1

MY VOYAGE TO D-DAY

My voyage to Normandy which began on D-Day was hilarious rather than heroic. I don't remember the name of the ship. It was a typically American one, something like Silas P. Finglestein.

She was one of a number of 'Liberty' ships that poured from the mass production lines when American industrial power became geared up for the war. Up till now she had been running between the American East Coast and the Clyde bringing war supplies to beleaguered Britain.

We gathered that the earnings from a round trip on these ships were so much that usually the crew left the ship when it docked back in the States and signed on with another one only when cash was running out. But this time when they docked in Scotland they found to their consternation that the ship was now under orders from the British Admiralty and was going on the invasion. That was how she came to be at Tilbury at the beginning of June 1944, waiting to embark the twenty four 25-pounders and their 'quads' (those oddly frog shaped four-wheel drive vehicles which pulled the guns and their limbers and carried the gun crew of six men and a substantial amount of ammunition) and the one hundred or so other trucks of 74 Field Regiment, Royal Artillery.

As a lieutenant in the regiment and having done a motor transport course, I had been given the job of supervising the loading of the guns and vehicles and I was to sail with them and the drivers. The gun crews and the rest of the men and officers of the regiment were to go on another ship to wherever we were going, and we were to meet up there.

There was some sort of industrial dispute going on in the docks when we arrived and I remember that we had to be very nice to the dockers and remind them that there was a war on and would they be kind enough to hoist our guns on board

The upper deck of one hold had been strung with hammocks for our drivers and the darkest corner of this part of the hold was screened off with a piece of hessian to form 'the officers' quarters'. There, a solitary hammock was hung for me. But soon after we went on board I was approached by the chief engineer, a lovely white-haired old boy who had spent his life at sea and had been recalled from retirement for the war and was one of the few members of the crew who really knew his job. I saw him as one of those croaky old grandfathers in a 'western', stoutly defending the homestead with a shot gun.

He said to me what sounded like "Got a cart in my cab'n". I said "What?". When on his repeating this I still couldn't understand him, he beckoned me to follow him and there in his day cabin he pointed to a camp bed. Differences of vocabulary and pronunciation in our common language had confused me. His cot, which is camp bed in English, sounded like cart to me. However you pronounce it, he was kindly offering it to me. So I slept comfortably on a 'cot' in the chief engineer's day cabin, used his hot shower and dined in style in the ward room with the rest of the ship's officers, while my poor men were confined to their hammocks in the hold with a solitary hose pipe to wash with.

They had only the army rations of that strictly rationed time to eat, though they did supplement them I gathered from the officers' 'trash'. We got the marvellous 'compo' rations which contained luxuries like tinned marmalade pudding only after we got ashore in Normandy and later - what was more of a luxury still - sliced white bread! (Bread at home in the war was made with 'national' flour of 70% extraction and was grey in colour - and probably very good for us). I in my exclusive heaven in this American ward room was introduced to breakfasts of bacon and maple syrup, as much of everything as you could eat and - best of all - the marvellous American coffee. I still think of it as the best coffee I ever had.

Because I suppose of the way they were recruited, they were an extraordinarily ill-assorted crew. The captain was English. He had been in the Royal Navy, had retired before the war and emigrated to the States and had taken up farming. He appeared to take no interest in the running of his ship and spent nearly all his time in his cabin where, we were told, he played bridge endlessly with whatever officers he could induce to join him

The first and third officers were respectively Russian and Spanish and rather poorly acquainted with the English language and the chief steward was German. This meant that the 'hands' who were mostly English speaking Americans were controlled - to the extent that they were controlled at all- by the second officer, the only one apart from the engineer who spoke English as a native. But he had nothing to do with the navigation and we never knew who, if anybody, was in charge on the bridge.

On the morning of the 6th of June we heard the dramatic but laconic BBC broadcast announcement: "Under the command of General Eisenhower, Allied naval forces supported by strong Air Forces began landing Allied Armies this morning on the northern coast of France", it said - but no hint at that time of whereabouts on that northern coast. In the afternoon Captain Hamilton, second in command of our battery, very handsome with a Clark Gable moustache, came on board to take charge of us. He was well known to have left his love behind in France when he was evacuated from Dunkirk in 1940. I have heard since the war that he found her again in 1944 and later married her. He brought orders which were not to be opened until we set sail. At about 6 o'clock in the evening we cast off from the dock and we gathered round Hamilton for this exciting moment of opening 'sealed orders'.

From the bulging brown envelope there emerged among other things a bundle of maps. We soon saw that these were of the coastline of Normandy - quite large scale ones - 1 in 100,000, about half inch to the mile. We were to land near the village of Le Hamel on D+2, 8 June. 151 Infantry Brigade, consisting of three battalions of the Durham Light Infantry, which our regiment always supported, were to be the reserve brigade and go in behind the other two brigades of our division which would land on D-Day - had in fact already landed by this time. The leading brigades were supported by regiments whose guns were self-propelled, mounted on tank chassis (they were called priests), and so could be brought into action more quickly than ours which were towed and had to be uncoupled from the quads and limbers (ammunition trailers) before they could be fired.

Soon after we had begun to move down the Thames - on the wrong side of the river - we were involved in a minor collision with a barge. We assumed somebody was steering but we weren't quite sure We really had no idea of what was before us; but I know I slept peacefully in my 'cot' until the next morning. It was a brilliant sunny day when I went on deck on D+1. We were now in a line of ships passing through the straits of Dover, hugging the English coast with a heavy smoke screen between us and the French side of the Channel. This was laid down to hide us from the long-range guns on the French coast. That was their real purpose from our side; but the Germans (it transpired later) assumed their purpose was to hide from their view the active preparations on the Kent coast for what they thought would be the real invasion. The smoke thus quite unintentionally acted to confirm the delusion they were under that this wasn't the 'real' invasion.

All that day we steamed along the Sussex coast and had still not turned towards France when we went to bed that night. Next morning we awoke to an astonishing sight. We were in a wide bay full of ships. I remember thinking how peaceful it all looked, like an enormous regatta. Lots of little boats were speeding between the big ships and the shore; and the one reminder that this was war - two battleships, Rodney and Warspite, were almost lazily loosing off their big guns every now and then. But the shells were landing somewhere way inland and we only occasionally heard the deep crump of their explosions. There were flights of aircraft overhead, but they were all OURS.

As we steamed slowly and apparently blindly towards the shore, a naval launch came towards us and shouted by megaphone for us to stop. There was nobody on our bridge, it seemed, so we carried slowly on our way and duly got our propellers entangled in an anti-submarine net. Now we had to stop and divers had to be summoned to cut us free.

Our sealed orders had told us that when we anchored off the French coast, Royal Engineers would come on board and unload our guns and vehicles, using the ship's derricks, into smaller craft for the run-in to shore. But now we received a signal to say that, owing to the tactical situation, priorities had changed and 7th Armoured Division would be unloaded before us. We must get ashore as best we could as no engineers would be coming to help. We turned to our ship's crew and said that we would do all the manual work if they would do the skilled job of working the derricks. However, this wasn't in their contract. After lengthy negotiations they agreed to do the job, but on a kind of work-to-rule basis with regular coffee breaks. We had to agree to this although it meant it took at least 36 hours to unload the ship. During one of these breaks the whole crew went ashore in the lifeboats to hunt for souvenirs and returned with some rather gruesome ones. They included a British colonel's battledress, presumably stripped off a corpse on the beach

The drivers of the small landing craft used for the ship-to-shore unloading operations were not highly trained. An anchor attached to the stern was supposed to be dropped just before they beached and by means of this they winched themselves off again when they had unloaded. Absurd tangles resulted with anchors failing to get a hold and then getting entangled in the cables of other craft. Some craft were held like this tantalisingly near the shore but not near enough to unload.

Several days before we left our last camp before Tilbury we had had to 'waterproof' all our trucks and quads in readiness for this adventure. They had to be able to drive through four feet of water without stopping or damaging the engines.

Marvellously detailed written instructions had been put together by somebody, specific for every type of vehicle. All sorts of vent holes had to be temporarily stopped with putty or sticky tape; corrugated tubes leading up above the bonnets were fitted to engine air intakes and exhaust pipes. Some of the holes had to be unblocked as soon as possible, others could be removed at our leisure, I particularly remember that the filler plugs on the batteries, which have breather holes, were to be fitted with condoms (What a waste! It was said) A carefully calculated supply was issued with no extras.

My Bedford 15 cwt. truck, which carried the troop wireless set and the equipment for directing the guns, was the last ashore from the Silas P., reaching dry land without any entanglement after an exciting plunge down the ramp into several feet of water. The waterproofing worked like a charm and the engine purred contentedly from under water. Off we drove through the sand dunes along clearly marked tracks, following the signs painted half and half blue and red (for artillery), carrying the number 42 (a code number for our regiment) and in the corner the black-on-red TT monogram 'twixt Tweed and Trent' for 'Fifty div' the 50th Northumbrian division.

So two days late we joined our comrades who had been waiting for us with an intense feeling of uselessness, huddled in a wood, with no guns. "Where on earth have you been?" they wanted to know. "A slight delay in America" we might have replied.

At once I resumed by normal duties of Gun Position Officer (GPO). My superior had already selected the field in which I was to get the four guns of my troop into action. But just then came the one moment of real panic I experienced in the whole war. Some soldiers came running round the bend of in the road in front of us saying "They've broken through!" I can remember now that physical feeling in the guts at the prospect that any moment a German tank might come lumbering round the corner. There was a moment of paralysis. Then discipline took over.

Our 25-pounders, though designed to fire over the heads of the infantry from positions well back from the front line, could in emergency be fired with what was called open sights. At point blank range with solid steel shot instead of explosive shells they would make short shrift of almost any tank. It was a drill we often practised. But before I had collected my senses and given the order for this, it became apparent that it was a false alarm. There had been no breakthrough.

British, 25-pounder

The line held and we proceeded to take on our normal role of firing indirectly at targets visible only from observation posts with the forward infantry. Panic over!

In fact we were not called upon to fire at all from that position. Later that evening we moved forward to a new position some half a mile to the south. I think we didn't fire at all from there either. Finally we moved again something like a mile to a point where I positioned the guns astride a rough track running east and west with gently rising ground ahead, that is to the south. Amazingly we stayed in that position for about six weeks. This was because there was little movement during that period - neither advance nor retreat - of the right hand part of Second Army's front which we were supporting, because the infantry, materially aided by the thousands of shells that we did fire from there, managed to see off an endless succession of counter-attacks.

This is what I recall happened to me. In the next chapters I outline the background to all this in the light of the history that I read after the event.

Chapter 2

THE NEED FOR A NEW ACCOUNT

Why yet another book about D-Day and Normandy? The need arises from the fact that all previous books and accounts have omitted the three factors which were vital to the Allies' success. They were, firstly:

Change

It was hardly mentioned that until January 1944 the plan for the invasion was the plan worked out by COSSAC, (acronym for Chief of Staff to the Supreme Commander, Designate), an Anglo-American planning team, presided over by the British General, Freddie Morgan, who had been appointed early in 1943 and had started work in May of that year. This plan was superseded in the first few weeks of January 1944 by a plan drawn up by Montgomery's staff after his return to England on his instructions. This was essentially a strengthening and widening of the COSSAC plan, as well as a total change in the command structure.

Luftwaffe

The second important omission from the accounts of D-Day and after was this: while recognising the overwhelming predominance of the Allied air power in western Europe compared with the German and the vital importance of this superiority, previous authors have failed to give the reason for this German weakness. The reason was that by this stage in the war the Luftwaffe had had to give up its traditional role of supporting the army because of the prior need for it to defend German cities against the devastating attack by British and American heavy bombers. The historians of this stage in the war have been most reluctant to admit any military gain to the Allies from the heavy bomber campaign. Only Richard Overy does so in his *'Why the Allies Won'*.

Allied air force

The third thing left out of account by the chroniclers of D-Day and after was again a matter of a plan superseded or sidelined, as it turned out to our great advantage. The plan was the decision that had been taken as to how the Allied air forces should be used to isolate the battle area and allow the invading armies to establish themselves ashore. This had been made at a meeting on March 25 convened by Eisenhower and was the 'transport' plan, as opposed to the 'oil' plan. It was to concentrate on preventing the Germans from bringing reinforcements to the front by mounting attacks on railway marshalling yards and repair depots as opposed to attacking pinch points of railways, which would be in Zuckermann's opinion too expensive. The other, the 'oil' plan making German forces short of oil was decided on.

Montgomery's part

While still commanding the British Eighth Army in Italy, Montgomery in the last months of 1943 had been appointed to command the land forces for OVERLORD under the overall command of General Eisenhower, 'Ike', who was designated SUPREME COMMANDER. Churchill sent the plan to Monty to study on his way home from Italy at Christmas 1943. Monty's very critical comment was that it was "not an operation of war". He was not alone in this opinion; but he was alone in having the courage and conviction, once he had the responsibility, to see that the plan was thrown out and a better one substituted. This was Montgomery's comment in his diary on the COSSAC plan :

The front of the assault was too narrow; only one corps HQ was being used to control the whole front; no landing was being made on the east side of the Cherbourg peninsula though the early capture of the port of Cherbourg was vital; the area of the landing would be very congested.

Having previously ascertained that neither Churchill nor Eisenhower liked the COSSAC plan, Monty on his arrival in England, told his very able team of staff officers who had been with him in Italy and in Africa to draft a new OVERLORD. It embodied a five-division assault (instead of COSSAC's three), flanked by airborne landings, and stretched from the River Orne in the east to the east side of the Cherbourg peninsula: a fifty mile wide beachhead.

With his experience he could see that the command structure too in the COSSAC plan would result in confusion. This also was changed, with separate British and American forces under separate British and American army commanders, and with separate lines of supply. The new plan was particularly welcome to General Omar Bradley whose role as commander of the United States First Army was changed. Under COSSAC Bradley was to have been in initial command of the whole operation; now he commanded the American army only.

The story of D-Day itself is well known. It was indeed a triumph; but so was the less well known story of what followed it - the Battle of

Normandy. Even less known than either is what came before. D-Day is what sticks in everybody's mind as a huge success; the gruelling and bloody but ultimately successful battle that followed it is hardly remembered.

Allied Plan of Campaign

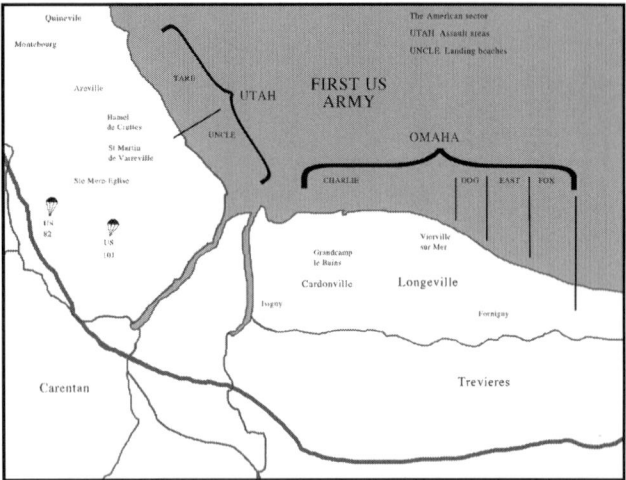

The American Sector

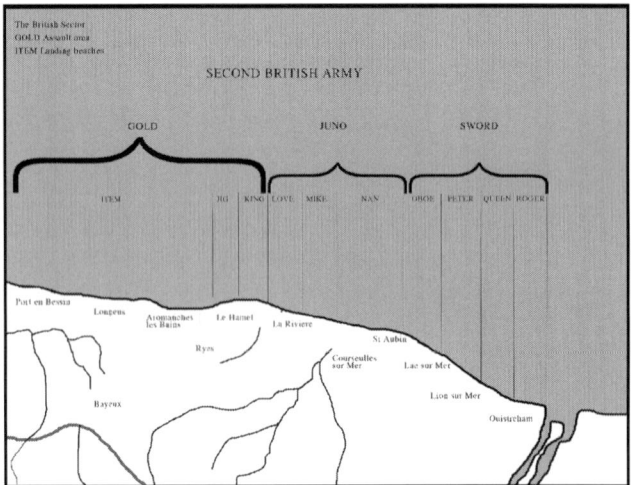

The British Sector

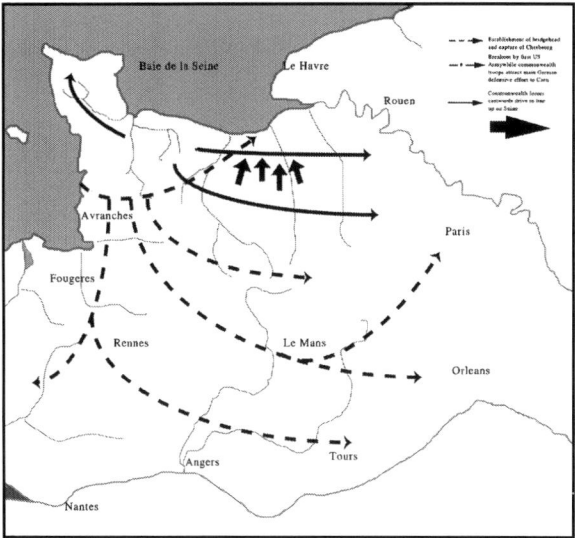

Original plan of April 1944

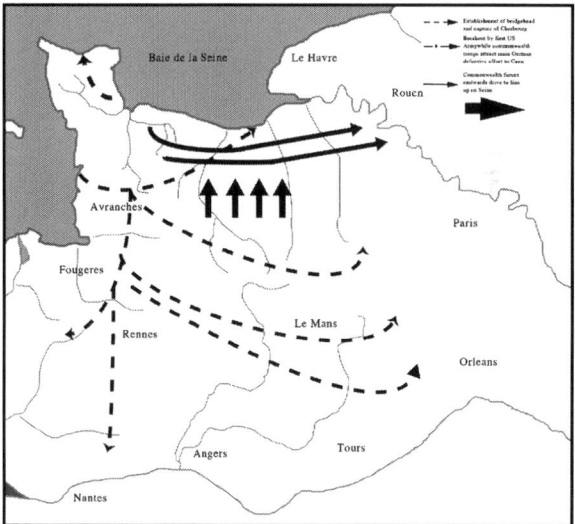

Revised plan, 7 May 1944

Chapter 3

WHERE THE WAR HAD GOT TO

When France surrendered to the Germans in June 1940, Germany was left in control of the whole European coastline. There was nowhere where a British army could directly attack the Germans. The only possibility for aggressive action was by means of a sea landing. Soon after the Americans came into the war, in December 1941, they began to agitate for such an attack; but the British were able to convince them that this would be foolhardy, and the disastrous Dieppe raid much later, in August 1942, in which the Canadian 2nd Division landed and suffered terrible casualties, confirmed this view.

So the allied attention was turned to the Mediterranean, the one area where, in the North African desert, there was military contact. The major operation decided on was code-named TORCH, an Anglo-American unopposed landing in north-west Africa. It took place on 8 November 1942, to coincide with a land offensive from Egypt at the other end of the Mediterranean coastline, at El Alamein the only place where British troops faced the Germans. The landings on the Mediterranean coast were launched from England and those on the west African coast directly from America.

This having been decided on, a cross-Channel landing in 1943 became impossible too. Most of the trained troops were committed in the Mediterranean and it was decided to use them by assaulting first Sicily - in July 1943 - and then the mainland of Italy in September that year.

OVERLORD planned

Spring 1944 was now the target date for a cross-Channel attack based in England; and in March 1943 the British general Freddie Morgan was appointed COSSAC (Chief of Staff to the Supreme Commander (designate), and started work in April to plan the operation. It wasn't until December 1943 that Eisenhower, at that time supreme commander in the Mediterranean, was appointed Supreme Commander for what was now called OVERLORD the cross-channel operation, and Montgomery under him Land Force Commander. Even the Americans, when it came down to it, realised that in the face of attacks by the V-weapons (the buzz bombs etc) on south-east England; an assault on the French coast was going to be a hazardous operation, and it is worth remembering that when it came to the morning of

6 June 1944 - D-Day itself - Eisenhower had in his pocket a communique which read:

Our landings in the Cherbourg/Havre area have failed to gain a satisfactory foothold and I have withdrawn the troops.

Failure of the Allies on D-Day would have enabled the Germans to develop to the full the suppression of Europe, more would have been done to death at Auschwitz and elsewhere; and the Germans would have been able to resist for far longer the Russian attack from the east. It is unlikely they would have been able to hold it off for more than a year or two; but when they were finally defeated, the Russians would have been masters of the whole of Europe, and the western Allies would have had no say in any part of it. France, Italy, the Low Countries - all would have fallen behind the iron curtain and suffered the fate that ultimately did befall East Germany, Poland, Hungary and all the countries that have now joined the EU. We would not have seen that splendid resurgence of western European democracy under those great leaders, Adenauer in Germany, de Gaulle France and de Gasperi in Italy, and the sixty years of peace in western Europe. Certainly there would have been nothing to celebrate sixty years on, as we are celebrating this June. (I wrote this on the occasion of the 2004 anniversary of D- Day).

Planning backwards

In his own account, Monty wrote that his approach was based on lessons that he had learnt: that it is necessary to plan backwards from the end to the means.

There must be a direct relationship between the two. The first need was to decide how operations on land were going to be developed and then to work backwards to ensure that we landed in the way best suited to the needs of the master plan.

Once a secure footing in Normandy was obtained, he wrote, *my plan was to threaten to break out on the eastern flank, that is the Caen sector. By pursuing this threat relentlessly I intended to draw the main enemy reserves, particularly his armoured divisions, into that sector and keep them there, using the British and Canadian forces (Second Army) under Dempsey for this purpose. Having got the main enemy strength committed on the eastern flank, my plan was to make the break-out on the western flank using for this task the American forces (First Army) under Bradley.*

So important was it to create the British-Canadian defensive shield to protect the US First Army against counter-attack that early in January Montgomery declared his intention of landing five brigade groups in the British sector, allowing only three to be put ashore in the American sector.

Hadn't the plans for 'OVERLORD' been worked out in great detail long beforehand by COSSAC? Yes, indeed. Morgan's plan, the result of one and a half years of research and discussion, was argued before Churchill, Roosevelt and a thousand senior generals, air marshals and admirals. None had confidence in it. That this plan for a 3-division assault was a recipe for disaster now seems undeniable. General Devers who was, until Eisenhower took over, commander of the American forces in Britain, was one of many who wanted an increase in the size of the assault. So did COSSAC itself. Through no fault of their own, they hadn't got the power to insist on the increase of scale which was vital.

Not only was the size of the invasion force too small but it committed the allies in Monty's opinion to the same error that had so nearly resulted in catastrophe in the landing at Salerno in Italy on 10 September 1943 and would, he rightly guessed, cause them to flounder when they landed higher up the coast of Italy, at Anzio, on 22 January 1944.

The error was the confinement of the invasion to one easily contained beachhead.

The change of Plan

Monty's new plan, OVERLORD inspired confidence in everybody. The fact that those in the know now believed in the plan, provided an infectious optimism that enthused those who actually had to do the job. All now looked forward to the invasion with tremendous optimism.

To a select few of those involved in the planning of OVERLORD, Montgomery's arrival back from Italy on 1st of January 1944 came as a kind of miracle. General Paget, who had been standing in as Land Force Commander pending Monty's appointment, used that very word.

What was done in the six months after Ike and Monty arrived was a Miracle of War

In fact Ike did not arrive in England (from a leave in the US) and did not convene a meeting until January 15. The meeting had before it the COSSAC plan and Monty's new plan; and it decided for Monty's. However much they might resent Monty's arrogant manner, they knew in their hearts that this was the very thing that was needed: a confident battlefield commander with

guts, experience, and the will to ensure that
OVERLORD succeeded.

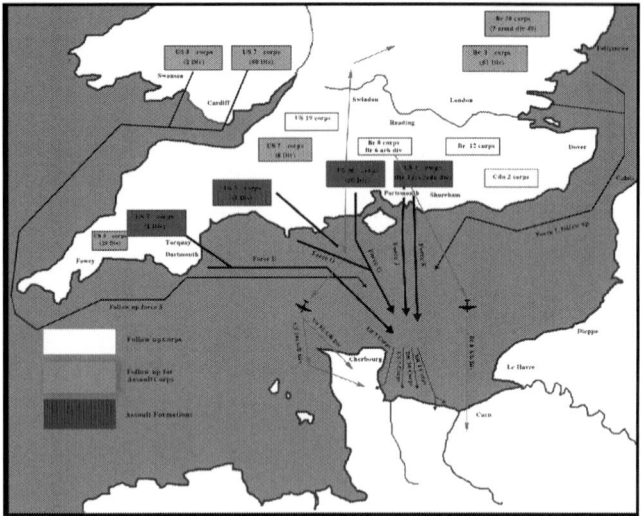

Operation OVERLORD

In the space of three days Monty's team
turned a recipe for disaster into a plan that had
every prospect of success, according to Nigel
Hamilton, Montgomery's biographer. The plan
was indeed ultimately successful. Brigadier 'Bill'
Williams (later Major General Sir Edgar Williams),
Monty's Chief Intelligence Officer who remained
his Chief of Intelligence for the rest of the war
said:

I came back to England shortly before Monty.

Various people had spoken of a landing on the Cherbourg peninsula (Utah beach). However the difference which Monty's arrival made was the incredible decisiveness which followed.

General Devers who was, until Eisenhower took over, Commander of the Americans in England, was one of many who wanted an increase in the size of the assault. So did COSSAC, but he had no power to insist on it. Until Monty came, nobody acted.

Misunderstandings

Both Churchill and Eisenhower felt the confidence and enthusiasm that radiated from Montgomery when his plan had been accepted. It was fully explained to them; but both were romantics where war was concerned. Neither took it in fully. Both had the idea that in order to win you had to go on advancing and that success was to be measured by the taking of territory. When it came to the point when there was no apparent progress on the ground both got worried. Eisenhower who had no experience of command in the field believed in attacking and making progress all along the line all the time. When Monty failed to achieve this, Ike got worried. When there was a period of stagnation he seriously entertained the idea that Monty should be replaced. This was just at the moment that Monty was preparing his coup de grace with the St. Lo break-out by the Americans. The chief mischief-maker was Air Chief Marshal Tedder, who in the superfluous post of deputy to the supreme commander, had nothing much else to do.

It was an exact repetition of what had happened at Alamein. On 27 October 1942 Churchill and some Ministers in London assumed that he was giving up from the fact that Monty had withdrawn from the line two British armoured divisions and the New Zealand division. Then too he was in fact preparing operation SUPERCHARGE his knock-out blow to Rommel's defences.

In Normandy after it was all over, Monty was asked when it was that he knew he had won.

When I was able to take three armoured divisions into reserve, he replied.

Opportunity Lost

In the subsequent histories much would be made of the speed of the advance of Patton's American Third Army which exploited the break-through made by Bradley's First Army. It was superbly done with great panache - but in fact it advanced no faster than did the British 30 Corps under General Horrocks, when in September it advanced from the Seine to Brussels and Antwerp in three days.

Patton's Army consisted of fresh troops and quite rightly avoided most of the fighting. 30 Corps comprised three British divisions which had all been heavily involved in the battle in Normandy. Tragically Eisenhower, who had now taken up overall command from Monty, halted them there in Belgium. Horrocks has said that when he reached Brussels on the 3rd or 4th September there was nothing to block his further advance northwards; and there were fleets of transport planes in England doing nothing but which could have been employed to supply him and Patton via Brussels airport; but on order from above he was halted. He thinks this was a critical moment of the war and a great mistake. If he had been allowed to go on, the war might well have been ended in 1944; but the moment of opportunity was fleeting. In a few days the Germans had regrouped and opposition was being organised. The chance of ending the war quickly was gone. The evidence that the panzer divisions disabled in

Some slightly over-optimistic forecasts were put out from Montgomery's HQ as to what the position might be at certain stages. It was hoped that Caen would be taken on D-Day. In fact it wasn't taken until the second half of July. It was hoped that soon afterwards the area between Caen and Falaise, flat and ideal for airfields, would be taken. This area was not actually taken until the battle was in effect won. In the end it wasn't necessary to have the airfields there. The RAF and USAF gave the army very adequate cover from England and the airfields constructed in Normandy nearer the coast.

What the bombers did

It is worth mentioning that the reason they were able to do this was that the German Air Force, the Luftwaffe, had been substantially broken by this time and what was left of it had to be used to defend Germany itself from the day and night onslaught on the cities by the British and American heavy bombers based in England. This heavy bomber campaign has had a bad press. The fact was that in spite of its immense cost in aircraft and manpower and inventive resources it forced the Luftwaffe into defending the German homeland and destroyed it there and so deprived the German army - in the west and in the east - of the air cover it had been trained to expect. This made it possible for the Russian armies to defeat the Germans and also for the Western Allies to pursue their military operations virtually unmolested from the air.

Preparing the people

Few commanders in history have recognised to such an extent the part played by the friends, relatives, wives and children of the soldier in battle. He was certain that Normandy would be the greatest western battle of the war; but it would only be won by men who felt their country was behind them.

He was aware that it would take a minimum of 2½ months of battle to reach the Seine, perhaps 3½. The soldiers must not feel that their relatives at home were disheartened when swift victory was not won. To mobilise the courage and perseverance of the soldier was not enough then; he must go out and mobilise the will of the nation itself.

As well as aiming to be seen in the months before D-Day by every soldier, British, American and Canadian who was to go on the invasion, Monty went out of his way to address a wide cross section of the British people: railway workers, factory workers and dockers, telling them of their vital part in the battle that was to come. The Director of Supply at the War office asked if he would sometimes go to the factories where there were bottlenecks in supply. He did.

Deception

The administrative plan that ensued was inspiring too. No little detail was overlooked in the equipping and bringing together of all those men, vehicles, ships and aircraft.

Added to all this, there were the touches of genius: the Mulberry harbours; PLUTO (the pipeline under the ocean, supplying petrol to the armies in Normandy); and the 'funny' tanks that swam ashore and bridged ditches. Above all, there was the achievement of surprise by means of ingenious deception plans, without which the operation would assuredly have failed. These so misled the enemy that they were not expecting an invasion then, and so did not look for it, enabling that immense armada to assemble in the Solent and then steam slowly to France without being noticed.

Although more than half the fighting men came from other countries, most of what I have mentioned was the work of the British. What we are entitled to celebrate is a quite unprecedented national feat of organisation, planning and cooperation, on an enormous scale.

Chapter 4

THE SURPRISE

At 9.30 in the morning of Tuesday 6 June 1944, the momentous announcement that the world had been waiting for was made from Supreme Headquarters Allied Expeditionary Force (SHAEF), Eisenower's headquarters and immediately broadcast by the BBC:

Under the command of General Eisenhower,
allied naval forces supported by strong
air forces began landing allied armies this
morning on the northern coast of France.

In Eisenhower's pocket at the time was another communiqué which fortunately never had to be issued (see page 22). And it ended with acceptance of total responsibility:

If any blame attaches to the attempt it is mine
alone.

The existence of this second draft communiqué is an important reminder that the success of D-Day was by no means assured beforehand. All those in the know realised that it was an unprecedented and extremely hazardous operation which would depend very much on good luck.

General Brooke, Chief of the Imperial General Staff, wrote in his diary on June 5:

> 'Very uneasy about the whole operation . . . it may well be the most ghastly disaster of the war.'

General Spaatz, commander of the United States strategic bomber forces in Europe, is on record as having said in March that year:

> 'This (expletive) invasion can't succeed, and I don't want any part of the blame. After it fails,' he added. 'We can show them how to win by bombing.'

But it did not fail because the luck held, especially the luck in regard to surprise.

Although the enemy, like the rest of world, were expecting an allied invasion of the continent, they were not expecting it there and certainly not then. And even after the invasion had happened on D-Day their leaders remained in two minds: was this the real thing or was it a feint, a decoy to draw attention and forces away from the real assault to be launched later elsewhere?

For more than a year the allies, mainly the British, had been operating a cover plan codenamed BODYGUARD containing a number of contributory sub-plans all with the general intention of causing the dispersal of enemy forces away from Normandy and away from the Russian front. The first element in this was to persuade the enemy intelligence services that our armies were much larger than they actually were. There was almost unbelievable success in this alone. In May 1944 German intelligence was crediting the allies with having assembled in Britain and neighbouring islands a total of from 85 to 90 divisions plus seven airborne divisions. The true figures were 45 plus 4. The belief in the existence of these large armies made it easy for the enemy to accept the existence of certain skeleton and wholly fictitious armies postulated by BODYGUARD,

The Germans kept sixteen divisions in Scandinavia (there were only seven in Normandy when we actually landed) against a supposed threat from the almost wholly imaginary 4th Army consisting of token British forces in Scotland and US troops in Northern Ireland and Iceland which, the double agents (who were the main sources of the disinformation) told them, were actively engaged on invasion exercises.

At the other extreme of the European coastline, the enemy maintained 24 divisions in the Balkans against the threat of an assault by the minimal British garrisons in Syria and Iraq, each blown up into an army, the 9th and 10th, and the wholly imaginary British 12th Army of six phantom divisions in Egypt. The planting of these armies on the enemy's intelligence maps was the work of Brigadier Dudley Clarke, probably the most brilliant and successful military illusionist.

In England itself preparations for invasion, of Europe, secret but not too secret, had for at least a year been going on in Kent to convey the idea that the invasion would be launched across the narrowest part of the channel against the French coast between Dunkirk and Dieppe. A skeleton group of armies with appropriate headquarters and the American acronym - FUSAG, First U.S.Army Group - was set up in Kent, purportedly under the command of General Patton, who was already well known and who allowed himself to be seen there from time to time together with his dog and probably also with his ivory-handled pistol. In fact of course he held a position one rung lower. He was to command the US 3rd Army, the reserve army whose role was to exploit, when the time came, the breach to be made in the German line by the US First Army under General Bradley. FUSAG was made up partly of imaginary divisions and partly of real ones destined for the follow-up in Normandy.

In April 1944 ostentatious preparations for invasion were made. Foreign diplomatic mail was censored and the south coast of England was sealed off. These moves were seen by the enemy as a too obvious signal that the invasion was imminent. That was intended. They were to serve to reinforce the more subtle hints that were also being dropped that the invasion could not be launched until late in July. Parties for foreign diplomats in British embassies abroad were suitable occasions for the dropping of these hints. Over drinks it would be "leaked" that everything was delayed by the hold-up in the supply of landing craft because of the (real) strike at Detroit, or General Montgomery's well-known reputation for refusing to attack until the last round of ammunition had been supplied was invoked to imply that, although everybody was exasperated with him, they had to give in and put it all off until July.

Operation COPPERHEAD

Operation COPPERHEAD was put on to confirm this idea in the enemy's mind. This was the charade in which Monty's double, the actor Clifton James, flew to North Africa via Gibraltar where it was certain he would be spotted by enemy agents. The notion being floated was that he was to confer with senior commanders in North Africa on the assault to be launched on the Mediterranean coast of France to draw the Germans there before OVERLORD. Of course an invasion of that part of France, operation DRAGOON, was carried out, but that was much later more than two months after D-Day. Americans landed near St.Tropez, unopposed and to no great purpose.

The famous double agents,as I've said,provided the principal means of conveying the false information which was always blended with innocuous truth. Thanks to Ultra (the code name given to the product of the code-breakers at Bletchley Park) it was often possible for the deception planners to see to what extent their bait had been swallowed, to drop the ploys that had been seen through and to reinforce those that were not. In general the principle was to tell the enemy what they expected to hear and to reinforce their preconceptions.

During the month before D-Day the impression that the invasion would be launched across the Straits of Dover was reinforced by the bombing policy. It was known that reports of every air raid were collated in Berlin. So for every bomb dropped in the real invasion area two were dropped north of the Seine. Finally when it came to the night itself, the enemy coastal radar station near Dieppe, the only one that had not been knocked out by bombing, was treated to a simulation of a fleet slowly advancing across the sea towards it. Aircraft flying in circles which moved slowly towards the French coast dropped strips of foil and produced this illusion on the screens.

The weather

The ultimate wholly unintended surprise was the weather. Eisenhower had laid down certain minimum condition of wind, waves and visibility. Since the middle of April the forecasters had been regarding each Thursday as D-Day and giving a forecast for it on the previous Monday.

The British forecasters were sure the task was impossible. In the English channel the weather is unpredictable more than two or three days ahead. The American were more confident. If the British could not forecast their own weather they would have do it for them. Group Captain J M Stagg of the RAF had the job of conducting a conference by telephone with the teams of British and American meteorologists, condensing the discussion into a consensus of opinion, and then presenting this to the Supreme Commander. As it turned out both teams were surprisingly successful in these trial runs; but this was because for the latter part of April and most of May the weather was reasonably fair and there were not many days on which a landing could not have taken place.

On the other side of the channel the German defenders remained on the alert against an invasion at any time. Then at the end of May the weather became unsettled. For some weeks Monday 5 June had been provisionally fixed for D-Day. It was the first of three days when the tides and the moon would be suitable. After that there would not be another concurrence for a fortnight. There had to be a late moon so that the paratroopers who were to be dropped at night could find their way about; and there had to be a rising tide at dawn.

The enemy defences were to be bombarded before the first landings, and this could be done only in daylight. The teams of engineers for demolishing the beach obstacles had to arrive on a rising tide so that they could do their work before the devices were covered by the high tide. This plan was responsible for a degree of surprise. Rommel expected the landings to be made at high tide and so regarded the 5th and 6th as unsuitable.

By the end of May the senior allied commanders (except for air) had moved from London to the Portsmouth area. Eisenhower, supreme commander, was at Southwick House and Montgomery, commander of the land forces, at the nearby Broomfield House. From now on they met, some fourteen of them - admirals, generals and air marshals, British and American, at intervals in the library at Southwick House. They met to hear the weather forecast. Everything else was by then settled in the smallest detail. The weather alone would determine the precise day.

On Friday, 2 June, the prospect was as unsettled as could be.

In all the charts for the 40 or 50 years that I had examined, Stagg afterwards wrote, *I could not recall one which at this time of year remotely resembled this chart in the number and intensity of depressions it portrayed.*

Nevertheless the 5th was provisionally confirmed as D-Day, pending further developments.

When the commanders and their chiefs of staff met under Eisenhower's chairmanship at 9.30 in the evening of Saturday, June 3, the prospects still looked bad and they decided to meet again at 4.15 on Sunday morning before taking an irrevocable decision. By that time all the assault convoys except those from Shoreham and the Portsmouth area had already sailed. There was no improvement in the forecast although the sky over Portsmouth at that time was clear. Stagg predicted that in four or five hours time a storm would blow up with wind and thick cloud; and he was right. He could give them no hope that they might avoid the approaching storm. Montgomery was for pressing on regardless; the majority were against. Eisenhower ordered a 24-hour postponement. The convoys already at sea were ordered to turn back to port.

At their next meeting at 9.30 pm on June 4, Stagg reported an unexpected development. There was now likely to be a brief period of better weather between two storms starting in the afternoon of Monday and lasting through the 6th; but it was unlikely that the conditions would reach the minimum asked for.

Provisional orders then went out naming June 6 as D-Day; but once again the commanders decided to leave it until the small hours to make the final decision. When they now met at 4 a.m. on Monday June 5th, Stagg confirmed that the improvement should last until June 8th. The commanders then made a unanimous decision to go. June 6 would be D-Day.

The commanders were naturally worried that they had no choice but to accept conditions worse than they had previously regarded as the minimum. But they could not know how much the bad weather would work out to their advantage. For the enemy, without any conference or serious discussion, called off the alert on the assumption that for the immediate future there was no possibility of invasion.

Stagg's ability to suspect on June 4th and confidently predict on the 5th that conditions on the 6th would be better depended on information which he had himself had to ask the navy to provide by sending ships specially and regularly to points way out across the Atlantic. The German forecasters were denied this information and so they were unable to see any possibility of a let up. If Stagg had been unable to foresee the lull between the storms or if Eisenhower had decided that they must insist on the originally agreed minimum conditions, the next target date would probably have been June 19. On the 17th the predictions for the 19th were reasonably favourable and the go-ahead for the 19th would almost certainly have been given.

But again there was an unexpected change, not a lull this time but a severe storm which broke on the 19th and lasted till the 22nd. It provided the worst weather on that part of the French coast in June in living memory. It was that storm which destroyed the Mulberry harbour on the American beaches and seriously damaged the British one.

Returning to the beginning of the month, the bad weather had the effect of a tranquilliser on the whole German command. The various headquarters were quite certain there would be no attack; and their confidence was boosted by the study that had been made of allied habits. All previous allied landings - which had all been in the

Mediterranean - had been made in fair weather.

Because of this attitude and of the weather itself, no German ship left harbour and no German aircraft made a reconnaissance of the English south coast on the vital days. But at the headquarters of the German 15th Army, guarding the Pas de Calais, there was great excitement when at 10.15 pm on June 5 the intelligence section heard this line, which they had been looking out for, broadcast by the BBC:

Blessent mon coeur d'une langueur monotone.

It was the second line of a poem by Verlaine. The first line had already been noted when it was broadcast on June 1. From captured underground sources they had discovered that the first line meant invasion within two weeks and the second line meant within 36 hours. Throughout that evening the BBC had broadcast other apparently meaningless statements:

It is hot in Suez. It is hot in Suez. And: *The dice are on the table. The dice are on the table.*

Each was repeated and each carried the instruction to carry out now some prearranged act of sabotage.

On the receipt of the Verlaine warning the 15th Army was ordered to stand to and the warning was sent back to Army Group B, Rommel's headquarters at La Roche Guyon on the Seine. But for some unexplained reason - one must assume the influence of the known anti-Nazi officers in that headquarters - they did not alert 7th Army which was defending Normandy.

And so the unbelievable happened. Some five thousand ships of all sorts and sizes assembled off the Isle of Wight on the Monday evening and proceeded to steam towards France in ten long slow columns all that night and yet they were not spotted until they dropped anchor in the Bay of the Seine at dawn on Tuesday. Even the minesweepers which came within a few miles of the French coast on the afternoon of June 5 were not spotted or at any rate not reported.

Field Marshal von Rundstedt, overall commander of the German forces in western Europe, never left his headquarters at St. Germain-en-Laye on the outskirts of Paris. But practically all the senior commanders under him down to 7th Army divisional commanders were for one reason or another away from their posts in the early hours of June 6. - most went to attend an anti-invasion exercise at Rennes in Britanny. Most conspicuous of the absentees was Rommel himself. His letters to his wife showed that during May he was in a constant state of indecision, oscillating week by week, between thinking the invasion imminent and being sure it would not come for some time.

At the beginning of June the weather forecast kept him in the latter state of mind for long enough for him to decide on a short leave in Germany. He wanted to see Hitler to persuade him to relinquish his personal hold on the two reserve panzer divisions within reach of the Normandy coast. If he went now he could be at home for his wife's birthday - June 6! He took her a pair of shoes from Paris and had just presented them when Speidel, his chief of staff, telephoned from France with the news of the invasion. There is some doubt as to precisely when this call was made; but it seems fairly certain that it was later than 9.30 am when the news was broadcast to the world by the BBC. Again there is the suspicion that the delay was deliberate. Speidel had in fact had a late night party for fellow anti-Hitler conspirators from among the staffs in the Paris area - *while the cat was away*.

Rommel listened without a word as Speidel talked and then he said:

How stupid of me! How stupid of me!

At once he prepared to drive back to France. Only after he had gone was it found that the shoes did not fit.

Rommel's absence from the scene on D-Day was crucial and the hardest to understand. With his experience of allied conjuring tricks and his views as to how the invasion should be countered, how could he have left his post without concrete evidence that the allies were not ready? He had been two days late for that critical battle, Alamein, the victim then as now of British deception. But for Normandy it was doubly important for him to be there on the day, because it was his strongly held view, not shared by von Runsted, that the best and probably the only chance of defeating the invasion would be to hit the invasion hard on the first day, on the beaches, before they could establish themselves ashore. It was Rommel who had said to a staff officer:

Believe me, Lang, the first twenty four hours of the invasion will be decisive and then, coining the title for a famous film: *For the allies as well as for Germany it will be the longest day.*

As unbelievable as the failure to detect the approach of the allied armada was what happened next. Although Hitler and his chief of staff Jodl guessed right, Rommel for one continued to believe that OVERLORD was a feint and that the real invasion would come later in the Pas de Calais. One would have thought that anyone who had witnessed the massive scale of the Normandy landings would have had to be out of his mind to think that the allies were capable of repeating them elsewhere and even more massively. That Rommel and others did think it was a triumph for the allied counter-intelligence but a lot was owed to the active anti-Nazis in the German intelligence. They passed on some of the allied "plants" with advantage - especially the exaggeration of allied strength.

On D+1 and on many succeeding days follow-up convoys from the Thames estuary and the east coast of England sailed through the straits of Dover on their way to Normandy. Smoke screens were laid to protect them from German artillery on the French coast and, even more important, the knowledge of them from the enemy. For had the Germans realised that troops and stores for Normandy were being embarked as far away as Felixstowe they would have been quickly relieved of the delusion that troop concentrations in Kent presaged an attack across the straits.

Quite unintentionally the smokescreens reinforced the enemy's delusion. They took it that the purpose was to prevent them from seeing the preparations for the invasion taking place on the Kent coast, and so their preconception that a Pas de Calais invasion force was to set off from there was confirmed!

On D+2, June 8, Hitler and von Rundstedt, over Rommel's head and probably against his will, ordered the movement of part of the 15th Army to Normandy. This was the cue for a spectacularly successful ploy by the double agent "Garbo". At a few minutes past midnight on June 9, Garbo contacted his controller in Madrid and transmitted a long and detailed situation report. The nub of it was that he and his three best (but entirely imaginary) sub-agents were sure that the Normandy operation was employing only a fraction of the forces gathered in southern England. In their opinion it was a diversion.

This report was immediately relayed to Berlin and from there to Hitler's headquarters at Berchtesgarten. It was brought to Hitler's personal attention at 10 pm. He then telephoned von Rundstedt and at 7.30 am on June 10 the movement order for 15th Army was countermanded. Next day Ultra decrypted a signal from Berlin to Madrid congratulating the "Garbo team" and asking to be told in good time of the target of the second invasion.

So for nearly six weeks, while the German 7th Army battered itself to death against the allied armies in Normandy and reinforcements were brought to it even from the Eastern front, Rommel kept his 15th Army almost intact and away from the battlefield, waiting for the real invasion that never came.

The account of the Battle of Normandy

Monty's overall plan was simple. We would capture a kind of baseline extending several miles inland from the beaches where we landed. The British would drive in a wedge on the left to form a shield to protect the Americans who would drive on Cherbourg and take the port and the whole peninsula.

So long as the British-Canadian left of the line in or near Caen could be held and attract the major part of the German forces, we were bound to win. As soon as the Americans were strong enough, they would attack and break through at St Lo and advance down to Avranches at the base of the Cherbourg peninsula, then wheel on the hinge at Caen with their right flank protected by the Loire, sweeping up the whole territory to the line of the Seine. Broadly speaking, this is what happened.

There were many checks on the way to success in Normandy. Eisenhower, among others got worried at the apparent lack of progress and even at one stage, blamed the lack of quick success on Monty and even wanted him to be sacked. Monty was happy so long as the main German strength was mounted against the Caen sector, that is against the Second Army. At one stage he had to act to keep it that way. He mounted operation GOODWOOD, a major attack that threatened to break out to the east of Caen and head for Paris. It was centred on three armoured divisions. It appeared to be a failure as Monty intended that it should look. It had his intended effect of bringing about the increase of German forces opposing the British and a compensating reduction of German strength opposing the Americans. It was closely followed by the American First Army's break out attack in the region of St Lo.

Most of the checks to allied progress were caused by dissensions and jealousies within the allied high command. In the COSSAC plan the breakout was to be made in the Caen sector, and as Morgan (who had himself been COSSAC) worked at SHAEF (Eisenhower's HQ), misunderstandings occurred. Progress was seriously held back by the great storm of June 17th - 19th, which destroyed the American Mulberry harbour and badly damaged the British one. There were operational difficulties too. The Americans took a long time to set the scene for the southward breakout and the British failed to take Caen and the country south of it. But this had its compensations. Monty had a great maxim that "*you cannot always get what you want in war. The important thing is to turn every setback into an advantage*". (It is incidentally a very good personal peacetime maxim too!) In this case the fact that after many weeks of heavy fighting the (British and Canadian) 2nd Army had been unable to enlarge its territory as much as intended meant that the Germans were that much nearer to the sea, and that meant that they could still be bombarded from the sea by the 15- and 16-inch guns of the British battleships, a devastating experience they never had in Russia or anywhere else.

The Breakthrough

After the war it was alleged by several historians that Monty's original intention was to break through near Caen and that the American breakthrough on the right was an afterthought necessitated by the stalemate at Caen, although there was documentary evidence to the contrary; and American historians alleged that it had been thought up by the Americans.

There was no intimation in the many accounts of D-Day and the associated events that there had been a change of plan. Few historians after the war paid attention to General Montgomery's role in this crucial change. In retrospect success seemed to have been inevitable. Basil Liddell

Hart, doyen of military historians of the period, made no mention of it in his *History of the Second World War* and Lord Alanbrooke, chief of the Imperial General Staff, effectively the head of the army, made no mention of it in his *War Diaries 1939 – 1945*. All write as if the plan used was in fact COSSAC's.

Chapter 5

THE AFTERMATH

The American breakthrough

On 25 July the American First Army's attack, operation Cobra, went in with conspicuous success. It was like the breaking of a dam. The first day the German front gave way a little. Then the Americans burst through. Patton's Third Army raced through the gap that had been created. Later, both American armies wheeled left and, to cut a long story short, after partly encircling and destroying the defeated German armies in the Falaise gap, by the end of August the Allied armies were lined up on the Seine, Canadians on the left, British in the middle and Americans on the right.

A few days later British armoured divisions had liberated both Brussels and Antwerp. They were part of Horrocks's 30 Corps which had made a spectacular dash from the Seine to the Belgian cities in three days. Horrocks (Edward Fox in the film 'A Bridge Too Far') was Monty's favourite general. He was now halted on orders from above, from Eisenhower who had by now taken over operational control of the combined armies from Monty. Horrocks was alleged to be outstripping his administrative resources. He was still being supplied by lorry from the Normandy beaches 300 miles away.

Lost opportunity?

Slightly over-optimistic forecasts were issued by Monty's headquarters, but there was one that turned out to be pessimistic. It was that the allies would line up along the Seine by D+90. In fact, victory in Normandy had been achieved well before that, and Horrocks's XXX Corps of the British 2nd Army had reached and taken Brussels and Antwerp on D+89, a hundred miles further on. Monty saw these dates only as guidelines, mainly for the benefit of the supply services.

Window of opportunity

Was there what we would now call a window of opportunity? A short time when the Germans were totally disorganised, reeling from the magnitude of their Normandy defeat before they sprang to their feet and reorganised? Horrocks certainly thought there was. He has said that when he reached Brussels on the 3rd or 4th of September, there was nothing to block his further advance northwards; but on orders from above, from Eisenhower who was now his immediate commander having now taken over command of the land armies from Monty, he was halted. He was alleged to be outstripping his administrative resources: he was still being supplied by road from the Normandy beaches 300 miles away. He thinks this was a critical moment of the war and a great mistake.

We had captured Brussels airport, he wrote. *If all those transport aircraft which had been sitting in the UK doing nothing could have been allowed to supply us (us being him and Patton, who was also raring to go), the war really would have been over in 1944.*

But the opportunity was fleeting. In a few days the Germans had regrouped and opposition was being organised. The transport aircraft were not immediately available; they were being assembled for Arnhem, MARKET GARDEN, which was launched a fortnight later on September 17th, not too little but already then too late.

The fortnight's delay before the complicated Arnhem operation could be launched proved fatal; for the enemy was growing stronger every day. The chance of ending the war quickly was gone.

If only

This is one of the great IF ONLYs. The possibilities of supply by air were fully shown to the world after the war was over, a few years later in the great Berlin

Air Lift when Berlin was cut off by the Soviets. To realise what an end in 1944 would have meant, one has only to think of what happened between December 1944 and the eventual end of the war in May 1945 - the many thousands of lives lost on all sides in that period and the added thousands fed to the gas chambers.

Heady days

I was myself there in Brussels in those heady days of early September 1944 when it really looked as if the war was almost over. I was in 50th (Northumbrian) Division, also part of Horrocks's corps. We had to deploy our 25-pounder guns (but luckily not fire them) in a public park where we were surrounded by admiring civilians who hugged us and kissed us and presented us with little gifts. We of course knew nothing of the problems of our commanders. We were just thrilled to be there after our exciting dash though northern France.

The hidden relief

We also knew nothing of the relief our arrival brought to a special section of those cheering crowds. In 1952, long after the war was over, I got to know a German Jewish girl Ursula Hertz, who had come to England after the war, having won a scholarship from a British textile firm as a designer. She and I discovered that we had been in Brussels at that same time, early September 1944, although of course totally unaware of each other's existence. She like many other Jews was in hiding in Brussels. Her father, in spite of having served with distinction in the German army in 1914, was like her in hiding. He had just been arrested, and now discovered, was on the point of being sent east; and she and her family – she was about eighteen at the time - had not dared to go out on the street until we came. For me, it was the high point of the war.

For her and her family, there were no words to describe their feelings when they realised that those tanks in the street were British and not German.

An account of Ursula's story is told by the same author in 'Ursula Sternberg. *Liberated in Holland, to flower in Philadelphia*', also published by Tricorn Books in 2011.

SOURCES

Major-General David Belchem, VICTORY IN NORMANDY

Nigel Hamilton, MONTY, Vols I,II,III Hamish Hamilton 1981-1986

Brian Horrocks, Belfield and Essame, CORPS COMMANDER, Sidgwick & Jackson, 1977

Richard Overy, WHY THE ALLIES WON, Cape